DISRUPTING INDUSTRIES

How Entrepreneurs Change the Game

LESLIE WATKINS

1

Table of Contents

CHAPTER ONE

Introduction

Disruption is reshaping industries and challenging norms in today's fast-changing business world. Entrepreneurial disruption can change how we live, work, and interact. Disrupting industries and entrepreneurs are explored in this introduction.

Disruptive innovation involves introducing new ideas, technologies, or business models that change an industry. It often involves finding market gaps and introducing faster, more efficient, and cheaper solutions. Disruptors upend the status quo, changing the industry and competitive landscape.

Visionary entrepreneurs who challenge conventional thinking drive disruptive innovation. These pioneers imagine new possibilities and push the limits of an industry. They combine creativity, resilience, and a relentless desire to change the world.

Entrepreneurs disrupt industries using various methods. They create disruptive products, services, and platforms using AI, blockchain, and the IoT. They reinvent value creation and delivery models. They track consumer behavior, trends, and preferences to meet market demands. Entrepreneurs also work with like-minded people, startups, and established companies to accelerate disruption.

Disruptive innovation offers great opportunities but also challenges. Industry incumbents may resist change to protect their vested interests and avoid disruption. Resource constraints and legal hurdles may slow disruption. Successful entrepreneurs overcome these challenges with strategic thinking, adaptability, and market knowledge.

Disruption affects many industries. It shapes economies, jobs, and social norms. Disruption boosts economic growth, employment, and innovation ecosystems. It also raises ethical issues like fairness, equity, and sustainability in rapid change.

We will examine case studies that demonstrate the power of entrepreneurial vision in disrupting industries. We will study industry disruptors like Uber, Airbnb, Tesla, and Netflix to learn from their successes and failures.

We will also discuss disruptive innovation trends, including emerging technologies and new disruption frontiers like healthcare and education. These trends can reveal industry transformation potential and entrepreneurial opportunities.

The entrepreneurial spirit that constantly challenges the status quo and reimagines what is possible disrupts industries. Entrepreneurs can transform industries, open new doors, and improve the game by embracing disruptive thinking and encouraging innovation.

CHAPTER TWO

Understanding Traditional Industries

Traditional industries have supported economies for decades, shaping our daily lives. These industries have a long history of economic growth and employment. Understanding traditional industries helps you understand disruptive innovation and its challenges and opportunities.

Traditional industries include agriculture, finance, healthcare, manufacturing, and transportation. These industries have long-standing hierarchies, processes, and market leaders. They follow time-tested rules and customs.

Characteristics of Traditional Industries

Traditional industries differ from disruptive ones. These traits illuminate industry dynamics and operational frameworks. Traditional industries have:

Existing players: Traditional industries have long-standing market leaders. Incumbents have brand recognition, market share, and extensive distribution networks.

Long-standing business models: Traditional industries have optimized processes and structures to maximize efficiency and profitability. These models usually follow best practices.

Physical assets and infrastructure: Traditional industries use manufacturing plants, machinery, warehouses, and distribution networks. These assets often require significant investment and can block new competitors.

Hierarchical organizational structures: Traditional industries have hierarchical organizational structures and clear decision-making processes. Ideas may need multiple approvals, which can slow innovation and agility.

Regulation and compliance: Traditional industries are regulated. Standards and regulations ensure safety, quality, and ethics.

Limitations and Challenges Faced by Traditional Industries

While traditional industries have their strengths, they also face limitations and challenges that make them susceptible to disruption. Some common limitations and challenges include:

Resistance to change: Due to entrenched practices, legacy systems, and a fear of disrupting revenue streams, traditional industries can resist change. This resistance can slow innovation and business model adoption.

Lack of agility and adaptability: Traditional industries may have trouble adapting to market changes. Their size, complexity, and rigid processes can make it difficult to respond quickly to changing consumer demands or emerging trends.

Siloed thinking and limited collaboration: In traditional industries, functional departments work independently on their goals. This siloed approach can hinder cross-functional collaboration and limit organizational knowledge sharing.

Inefficient processes and legacy systems: Traditional industries may use outdated systems or inefficient processes. Inefficiencies can raise costs, delay responses, and lower competitiveness.

Market saturation and intense competition: Traditional industries may reach market saturation, where existing players struggle to find growth opportunities. Established competitors can cause price wars and lower profit margins.

Opportunities for Disruption in Traditional Industries

Despite their limitations and challenges, traditional industries offer significant opportunities for disruption. These opportunities arise from various factors, including:

Unmet consumer needs: Traditional industries may have unmet consumer needs or underserved markets. These gaps and innovative solutions can change market dynamics.

Technological advancements: Artificial intelligence, blockchain, and the Internet of Things can be used to disrupt traditional industries. Automation, data analytics, and connectivity improve operations and add value.

Changing consumer behavior and expectations: Disruptive entrepreneurs can capitalize on consumer preferences for personalized experiences, convenience, sustainability, and digital interactions.

Regulatory changes or market reforms: Regulations or market reforms can allow new entrants or alternative business models. These changes can lower entry barriers and spur disruptive innovation in traditional industries.

Collaborative ecosystems: Startups, established companies, research institutions, and investors can collaborate to disrupt traditional industries. Partnerships, joint ventures, and accelerators enable knowledge sharing, resource pooling, and disruptive solution development.

Entrepreneurs can challenge established players, reshape traditional industries, and make meaningful change by seizing these opportunities. Disruptive innovation in traditional industries can open new growth paths, improve efficiency, and transform society.

CHAPTER THREE

The Role of Entrepreneurs in Disrupting Industries

Entrepreneurs shape industries and disrupt innovation. Vision, creativity, and willingness to challenge the status quo drive change. Entrepreneurs disrupt industries and change business in this introduction.

Entrepreneurs spot opportunities and launch new products, services, or businesses. They are resilient, risk-takers, and driven to change the world. Entrepreneurs innovate by thinking outside the box.

Definition of Entrepreneurship and its Importance

Entrepreneurship involves spotting opportunities, taking risks, and building new businesses. It is proactive, willing to challenge the status quo, and driven to transform. New ideas, technologies, and business models from entrepreneurs disrupt industries and change the competitive landscape.

Entrepreneurship disrupts industries. Entrepreneurs drive innovation and growth. They bring new ideas, innovative solutions, and the ability to spot industry gaps. Disruptive ideas and ventures increase competition, market dynamics, and customer value.

Entrepreneurship also generates jobs and growth. Successful startups create jobs and boost the economy. Entrepreneurs inspire others to innovate and start their own businesses, fostering creativity and resilience.

Traits and Skills of Disruptive Entrepreneurs

Disruptive entrepreneurs possess a unique set of traits and skills that enable them to challenge the status quo and bring about industry transformation. Some key traits and skills include:

Visionary mindset: Disruptive entrepreneurs see the future clearly. They can see possibilities others miss. Their vision drives their disruptive ideas.

Creativity and innovation: Innovative disruptors are creative. They excel at unconventional thinking, problem-solving, and challenging norms. Their innovative ideas disrupt industries and create new value propositions.

Risk-taking and resilience: Disruptive entrepreneurs like calculated risks. They embrace uncertainty to pursue disruptive ventures. They also persevere and learn from failures.

Adaptability and agility: Disruptive entrepreneurs can adapt to fast-changing markets. They can quickly adapt their strategies, business models, and operations to changing customer needs and market dynamics. In a fast-paced business environment, their agility lets them capitalize.

Leadership and networking: Leaders and networkers, disruptive entrepreneurs. They can motivate, build diverse teams, and communicate their vision. They use their networks to access resources, collaborate with like-minded people, and gain support for disruptive initiatives.

Case Studies: Successful Entrepreneurs Disrupting Industries

Numerous successful entrepreneurs have disrupted industries and left a lasting impact on the business world. Here are a few noteworthy case studies:

Steve Jobs (Apple): Steve Jobs' iPhone and iPad revolutionized technology. His vision for user-friendly, attractive devices disrupted the mobile and computing industries, changing how people use technology.

Elon Musk (Tesla, SpaceX): Tesla introduced electric cars and promoted sustainable transportation under Elon Musk. SpaceX transformed space exploration and satellite launches.

Reed Hastings (Netflix): Reed Hastings disrupted the entertainment industry with Netflix, pioneering the concept of streaming services and changing the way people consume movies and TV shows.

Brian Chesky (Airbnb): Brian Chesky disrupted the hospitality industry with Airbnb, creating a platform that connects travelers with unique accommodation options, challenging traditional hotels.

These entrepreneurs demonstrated disruptive abilities. They identified market gaps, challenged norms, and introduced innovative solutions that transformed industries.

Aspiring disruptors can learn the strategies and mindset needed to make a big impact in their industries by studying these case studies and successful entrepreneurs.

CHAPTER FOUR

Identifying Opportunities for Disruption

Identifying disruption opportunities is essential to transforming industries. Disruptive innovation can be found in inefficiencies, unmet needs, and untapped markets. This introduction discusses the importance of identifying disruption opportunities and the key factors involved.

Traditional industries can be disrupted if their practices and business models no longer meet market demands. Entrepreneurs can identify disruption opportunities by understanding these industries' constraints. They can then use their creativity, market insights, and entrepreneurial skills to innovate and challenge the status quo.

Analysis, observation, and foresight are needed to spot disruptions. Entrepreneurs must research market trends, industry pain points, and gaps in existing solutions. Entrepreneurs can find disruptive ideas, technologies, and business models by understanding customer needs and market dynamics.

Market Analysis: Identifying Existing Industry Gaps

Disrupting industries requires finding disruption opportunities. Entrepreneurs can find disruptive innovation by identifying inefficiencies, unmet needs, or untapped markets. We'll discuss the importance of identifying disruption opportunities and the key factors in this introduction.

Traditional industries' practices and business models may no longer meet market demands, creating disruption opportunities. Understanding these industries' limitations and challenges helps entrepreneurs identify disruption opportunities. They can then use their creativity, market insights, and entrepreneurial skills to challenge the status quo and innovate.

Disruption opportunities are found through analysis, observation, and foresight. Market research, industry trends, and pain points or gaps that existing solutions don't address are essential for entrepreneurs. By understanding customer needs and market dynamics, entrepreneurs can find opportunities to introduce disruptive ideas, technologies, or business models.

Technological Advances: Enablers of Disruption

Technology drives disruption. Entrepreneurs who stay abreast of emerging technologies can spot disruptive innovation opportunities. AI, blockchain, IoT, and data analytics can improve efficiency, enable new business models, and create new value propositions.

Entrepreneurs can find disruptive products, services, and processes by tracking technological trends and their applications. Technology can improve operations, customer experiences, and market creation. Tech-savvy entrepreneurs can spot and capitalize on disruption opportunities.

Consumer Behavior Shifts: Recognizing Changing Trends

Consumer behaviors reveal disruption opportunities. Entrepreneurs can fill market gaps by recognizing changing trends and consumer preferences. Consumers want convenience, personalization, sustainability, and digital experiences.

Understanding consumer behavior changes allows entrepreneurs to create disruptive business models that meet these needs. This could involve using technology to personalize services, offering sustainable alternatives, or reimagining traditional processes to improve convenience and digital interactions. Entrepreneurs can disrupt industries by meeting consumer expectations.

Market analysis, technological updates, and consumer behavior changes are needed to find disruption opportunities. Entrepreneurs can find industry gaps and inefficiencies by researching markets, using new technologies, and understanding customer needs. This knowledge allows them to create disruptive innovations, challenge norms, and create customer value. Entrepreneurs can disrupt their industries by adopting these strategies.

CHAPTER FIVE

Strategies for Disrupting Industries

Entrepreneurs who want to disrupt industries, innovate, and change business landscapes need strategies for disruption. Entrepreneurs can transform industries by using effective strategies. This introduction will discuss strategic approaches to disrupting industries and successful disruptors' strategies.

Business Model Innovation: Creating New Value Propositions

Disrupting industries requires business model innovation. Entrepreneurs can challenge norms by rethinking or creating new business models. New revenue streams, cost optimization, and unique customer experiences are part of business model innovation.

Entrepreneurs must assess the industry value chain, find inefficiencies, and consider alternatives. Disruptive business models like subscription-based services, sharing economies, and platform-based marketplaces allow entrepreneurs to create new customer value propositions and differentiate themselves from incumbents.

Leveraging Technology: Harnessing the Power of Innovation

Business model innovation disrupts industries. Entrepreneurs can introduce new value propositions and challenge norms by reimagining or creating new business models. Business model innovation involves finding new revenue streams, optimizing cost structures, and providing unique customer experiences.

Entrepreneurs must examine the industry value chain, find inefficiencies, and consider alternatives. Entrepreneurs can differentiate themselves from incumbents by introducing disruptive business models like subscription-based services, sharing economies, or platform-based marketplaces.

Disruptive Marketing: Reaching and Engaging New Audiences

Disruptive marketing strategies attract new audiences and challenge industry leaders. To reach their target market, entrepreneurs must use unconventional marketing methods like social media, influencers, and viral campaigns.

Disruptive marketing involves creating unique and compelling brand stories, using guerrilla marketing tactics, and leveraging user-generated content. By challenging traditional marketing channels and utilizing innovative strategies, entrepreneurs can generate buzz, build brand awareness, and attract new customers who resonate with their disruptive value propositions.

Collaboration and Partnerships: Accelerating Disruption

New audiences and industry incumbents require disruptive marketing strategies. Digital platforms, social media, influencers, and viral campaigns must be used by entrepreneurs to reach their target market.

CHAPTER SIX

Overcoming Challenges in Disrupting Industries

Entrepreneurs face many challenges when disrupting industries. Entrepreneurs must overcome obstacles to change business landscapes and innovate. This introduction will discuss the importance of overcoming challenges in disrupting industries and key strategies to overcome them.

Regulatory and Legal Hurdles

Startup founders facing legal and regulatory barriers to entry face a significant challenge. Barriers to entry and stifled innovation can result when established rules aren't adapted to accommodate new business models or technologies. To overcome these obstacles, you must actively engage with regulatory bodies, advocate for necessary changes, and have a firm grasp of the applicable legal framework. Entrepreneurs have the responsibility of understanding and meeting all applicable compliance requirements, applying for and receiving all required regulatory approvals, and working to create enabling regulatory frameworks that promote innovation and disruption.

Resistance from Incumbents

Entrepreneurs who attempt to disrupt established industries often face resistance from the established players in those industries. It's possible that well-established businesses will try to slow down disruptive innovations because they see them as a threat to their market share. To overcome this opposition, it is necessary to talk to people, work together, and show how good disruption is for the industry as a whole. Entrepreneurs have to network with people in their field, demonstrate the worth of their innovations, and talk up the ways in which disruption can bring about positive change and open up new opportunities.

Funding and Resource Constraints

Limitations in available funds and resources can pose serious challenges to the disruptive process. In addition to difficulties in gaining access to the people, resources, and physical facilities they need to bring their innovative ideas to fruition, entrepreneurs frequently face financial constraints. The only way to get past these roadblocks is to get creative and work together strategically. To maximize their impact, entrepreneurs must actively seek out investors who share their disruptive vision, investigate alternative funding sources, make use of shared resources and collaborative ecosystems, and optimize resource allocation.

Managing Disruption: Balancing Risk and Reward

Entrepreneurs who seek to disrupt established industries must weigh the potential benefits against the dangers involved. Due to the inherent risk in disruptive businesses, founders need to take a strategic approach, perform extensive market research, and iterate their plans in response to customer feedback. Entrepreneurs need to be adaptable and quick on their feet, willing to try new things and change course if necessary. Entrepreneurs can increase their chances of success and reap the benefits of disruptive innovations if they take risk management seriously.

Conquering obstacles is essential for bringing about industry disruption. Disruptive entrepreneurs face many challenges, including dealing with the law and regulations, dealing with incumbents who are resistant to change, dealing with limited resources, and managing the risks associated with their venture. Entrepreneurs can overcome these obstacles and drive transformative change within their target industries by actively engaging with regulatory bodies, building alliances, seeking innovative funding approaches, and adopting a strategic mindset.

CHAPTER SEVEN

Impact of Disruption on Industries and Society

Industry and society alike are being reshaped by the rising power of disruption. Disruptive innovations have an effect across multiple sectors, including business, society, and culture. The profound effects of disruption on industries and society will be discussed in this introductory piece, along with the opportunities and challenges that arise as a result of this revolutionary process.

Economic and Job Market Effects

Disruption has far-reaching effects on the economy and the job market, among other areas of society. Market dynamics, revenue streams, and employment patterns are just some of the ways in which disruptive innovations can alter established sectors. Disruption can be a source of innovation and economic growth, but it also has the potential to cause job losses and necessitate retraining.

Businesses may be able to offer their wares at reduced prices as a result of the productivity gains, efficiency enhancements, and cost savings made possible by disruption. These gains in efficiency, however, may come at the expense of some occupations and even entire markets. Investing in reskilling and upskilling programs, encouraging entrepreneurship, and creating a climate that encourages career transitions are all important ways to mitigate the potential negative effects of disruption on workers.

Changes in Consumer Behavior and Expectations

Consumers' habits and expectations are significantly shifted by disruption. Consumer tastes can be rapidly reshaped and established market segments disrupted by innovations that offer greater convenience, personalization, and affordability. Customers nowadays anticipate sustainable business practices, on-demand services, and a seamless digital experience.

The elimination of middlemen is made possible by disruptive technologies and business models. There has been an increase in consumer agency, information availability, and freedom of action. Businesses need to use data analytics, AI, and other technologies to track shifting customer preferences.

Social and Environmental Implications

The social and ecological effects of disruptions must be carefully considered. Although it has the potential to bring about positive social change by resolving problems, broadening participation, and expanding access to resources, it also has the potential to deepen existing inequalities and destabilize established social order. Privacy issues, data security, and the fair treatment of gig economy workers are just a few examples of the ethical dimensions of disruption that must be addressed.

Further, change can be a driving force for environmental sustainability. Clean energy innovations, resource efficiency tools, and circular economy strategies all help lessen the blow of global warming. To ensure that disruption is consistent with long-term environmental goals, businesses must adopt sustainable practices, develop eco-friendly products, and adopt responsible approaches.

Balancing Disruption and Sustainability

Long-term societal health requires striking a balance between innovation and long-term viability. Disruption presents promising openings for growth and development, but it needs to be conducted in accordance with ethical standards of sustainability and responsible enterprise. Frameworks that encourage sustainable disruption, advance circular economy models, and guarantee social and environmental responsibility should be developed jointly by entrepreneurs, businesses, and policymakers.

Businesses can benefit both their shareholders and society if they adopt a more sustainable approach to their disruptive strategies. They have the potential to create environmentally friendly methods of doing business, support programs with a positive social impact, and aid in the realization of global sustainability targets like the SDGs set by the United Nations (SDGs).

Disruption has far-reaching effects on industries and society as a whole. The economy, employment, consumer habits, social order, and ecological stability are all impacted. While changes in the status quo can lead to new discoveries and advancements, there are also risks that must be mitigated with caution. Harnessing disruption's transformative power to create a more inclusive, sustainable, and prosperous future requires understanding and addressing its economic, social, and environmental implications.

CHAPTER EIGHT

Ethical Considerations in Industry Disruption

It is essential to examine and address the ethical considerations that arise from the rapid pace of industry disruption, where new technologies, business models, and innovations are constantly reshaping markets. While disruption has the potential to bring about great improvements and changes, it also poses serious ethical questions that should be given careful consideration before any action is taken.

The range of stakeholders affected by ethical considerations in industry disruption includes workers, customers, communities, and the environment. Fairness, justice, privacy, sustainability, and the ethical application of technology are all touched upon here. In order to ensure that disruptive innovations are consistent with ethical norms and values, it is necessary for entrepreneurs, businesses, policymakers, and society at large to critically evaluate their ethical implications.

Responsibility and Accountability of Entrepreneurs

Entrepreneurs are crucial to driving innovation and shaping the future of business in the context of industry disruption. In this position, one must take full responsibility for the results of one's disruptive actions and give due weight to ethical considerations. Successful ethical entrepreneurs weigh the costs and benefits of their actions and make decisions that are consistent with their values.

A proactive approach to ethical decision-making that takes into account the effects of an entrepreneur's innovations on their staff, customers, neighbors, and the planet is essential. Fair employment practices are ones that discourage discrimination and bias in the workplace and protect individuals' right to privacy and confidentiality of their personal information. Entrepreneurs can help create a more moral and long-lasting landscape of disruption if they take personal responsibility and hold themselves accountable.

Ensuring Fairness and Equity in Disruption

Existing inequalities in society may be exacerbated by disruption or helped by it. Maintaining a level playing field during the disruption process and after the fact is essential. Examining how marginalized communities, vulnerable populations, and workers impacted by job displacement may be affected by disruptive innovations is an ethical consideration.

Business owners and executives have a responsibility to work toward eliminating inequalities and expanding access to opportunities. This involves working with community stakeholders to identify and mitigate potential negative effects, as well as promoting diversity and inclusion within their workforce. Disruption has the potential to bring about positive social change if it is guided by principles of fairness and equity.

Ethical Challenges and Potential Solutions

Disrupting an industry is fraught with moral difficulties. Ethical decision-making and responsible innovation depend on being able to recognize and address these obstacles. Privacy issues, data security, employment effects, environmental impact, cultural preservation, and data veracity are just a few examples of the frequent ethical challenges that arise.

Entrepreneurs can use a wide range of tactics to triumph over these difficulties. Ethical impact assessments are used to foresee and lessen negative consequences; decision-making processes are open and inclusive; stakeholders are consulted in the development of ethical guidelines and best practices; and a culture of ethical awareness and accountability is encouraged. Ethical frameworks, seeking advice from experts, and learning from past experiences are all ways to better deal with these difficulties.

The development of ethical guidelines and standards, as well as the collective solving of problems, can benefit from encouraging collaboration across sectors among business leaders, government officials, civil society organizations, and academics. By combining their insights, people can better understand ethical dilemmas and develop a culture of responsible disruption and constant improvement.

Entrepreneurs can make sure their innovations have a long-lasting, positive effect on society if they take ethical concerns into account during the process of disrupting existing industries. The principles of responsibility, fairness, and accountability are essential to ethical business practices. Entrepreneurs can effect positive change while adhering to the highest standards of ethics and social responsibility in the face of the disruptive environment if they make decisions consciously, work together, and remain committed to their ethical values.

CHAPTER NINE

Case Studies: Disruptive Entrepreneurs and Industries

Uber: Transforming the Transportation Industry

The transportation industry has been completely upended by Travis Kalanick and Garrett Camp's 2009 startup, Uber. Uber is an on-demand ride-hailing service that revolutionized the taxi industry by harnessing the potential of mobile technology and the sharing economy. Uber's easy-to-use app matched riders with private drivers, who in turn offered cheaper fares, more availability, and more streamlined service.

There were many obstacles in the way of Uber's disruptive business model, such as red tape and pushback from the taxi industry. However, its rapid global expansion can be attributed to its ability to capitalize on shifting consumer behavior and fill voids in the market. After Uber's meteoric rise, numerous competitors entered the market, altering the face of transportation and posing new challenges to the status quo.

Airbnb: Revolutionizing the Hospitality Industry

In 2008, Brian Chesky, Joe Gebbia, and Nathan Blecharczyk launched Airbnb, a website that allows people to rent out their homes or extra rooms to tourists. Airbnb was a game-changer for both hosts and guests because it tapped into the sharing economy to offer alternative lodging options to the standard hotel.

Regulatory scrutiny, safety and legal compliance worries, and pushback from the hotel industry were all obstacles Airbnb had to overcome. However, its novel approach to lodgings found favor with vacationers looking for off-the-beaten-path adventures. Airbnb has rapidly expanded into a global hospitality powerhouse, disrupting the hotel industry and fundamentally altering the way in which people travel.

Tesla: Disrupting the Automotive Industry

The automotive industry has been shaken up by Tesla, led by the visionary entrepreneur Elon Musk. Tesla has transformed the public's view of EVs and presented a formidable challenge to the conventional automobile industry by placing a premium on eco-friendly modes of transportation. Tesla has pushed the limits of what electric vehicles are capable of by combining innovative design, state-of-the-art technology, and a dedication to renewable energy.

There were many obstacles Tesla had to overcome, such as the high cost of producing electric vehicles, a lack of charging stations, and the resistance of established automakers to change. Tesla, on the other hand, grew rapidly thanks to its dedication to innovation, sustainability, and the creation of practical long-range electric vehicles like the Model S and Model

3. The disruptive nature of Tesla's approach has encouraged other automakers to invest in electric vehicles, hastening the advent of a greener transportation era.

Netflix: Changing the Entertainment Landscape

Netflix, which was started in 1997 by Reed Hastings and Marc Randolph as a DVD mail-order service, revolutionized the film and television business by being an early adopter of online streaming. Netflix challenged the status quo of cable TV and DVD rental services by providing instant, online access to a vast library of movies and TV shows.

Competitors in the industry were skeptical of Netflix, and the company had trouble securing the rights to distribute its content.

However, Netflix became a dominant force in the entertainment industry by capitalizing on technological developments and investing in original programming, such as the critically acclaimed series "House of Cards" and "Stranger Things."

Netflix is now a worldwide streaming powerhouse that influences consumer taste and forces established media companies to change their tactics. As a result of its innovative business model, competing streaming services have proliferated, causing a sea change in how people access and enjoy media.

These examples show how disruptive entrepreneurs can completely transform entire markets. These businesspeople shook up the status quo by introducing novel business models, technologically-driven solutions, and a keen awareness of shifting consumer preferences. Their achievements show the potential of disruptive thinking to revolutionize entire industries and improve the quality of life for everyone.

CHAPTER TEN

Future Trends in Industry Disruption

Exploring the future trends that will shape industry disruption is crucial as the business landscape continues to change at a breakneck pace. Successfully navigating the challenges and opportunities introduced by disruptive forces requires that business owners, executives, and policymakers anticipate these trends.

Technology development, shifting consumer preferences, and the call for more inclusive and sustainable business practices are all factors that will continue to shape the future of industry disruption. The industries they influence, the markets they birth, and the way society functions could all be drastically altered by these tendencies. Businesses can prepare for tomorrow's disruptive environment by recognizing and responding to these trends.

Emerging Technologies and their Disruptive Potential

Emergence and adoption of transformative technologies are intrinsically linked to the future of industry disruption. Industry landscapes will be radically altered as a result of developments in areas such as artificial intelligence (AI), machine learning, robotics, the blockchain, the Internet of Things (IoT), and quantum computing. New business models, improved customer experiences, and radical process improvements are all possible thanks to these technologies.

Examples of AI and ML include the ability to automate tasks, facilitate predictive analytics, and drive individualized service delivery. The automation and efficiency gains in the manufacturing, logistics, and service sectors are among the most promising applications of robotics. The distributed ledger technology known as blockchain has the potential to usher in a new era of trustworthiness and transaction efficiency. The Internet of Things (IoT) links gadgets together so that information can be tracked, monitored, and improved in real time.

To stay ahead of the competition and take advantage of new growth and innovation opportunities, businesses need to recognize and capitalize on the disruptive potential of emerging technologies.

The Rise of Sustainability-Driven Disruption

Future disruption in industries will be shaped in large part by sustainability concerns. The need for eco-friendly methods, goods, and services is rising as people become more aware of their impact on the planet. Sustainable businesses are in a prime position to take advantage of this shift and lead the way in industry innovation.

The adoption of circular economy principles, the incorporation of renewable energy sources, and the rethinking of traditional business models all contribute to sustainability-driven disruption. It entails a commitment to social and environmental responsibility as well as the development of environmentally friendly products. Businesses can win the patronage of environmentally conscientious customers, expand into untapped markets, and build long-term value by orienting their operations around sustainability objectives.

New Frontiers for Disruption: Healthcare, Education, etc.

Disruption will continue to occur in new and different industries in the future. Opportunities to reshape conventional models and address long-standing challenges exist in service industries such as healthcare, education, and others.

Disruptive entrepreneurs in the healthcare sector can use telemedicine, AI-powered diagnostics, personalized medicine, and remote monitoring to expand patients' access to care, boost health outcomes, and reduce healthcare costs. Similarly, education is undergoing a revolution thanks to the development of personalized and accessible online learning environments, adaptive technologies, and lifelong learning solutions.

Entrepreneurs, businesses, and policymakers must be willing to change, to question established ways of thinking, and to adopt novel strategies to meet the needs and expectations of an increasingly diverse consumer base.

CONCLUSION

Entrepreneurs are crucial to the process of industry transformation and innovation. They have the potential to upend established ways of doing business through their bold ideas, perseverance, and willingness to shake things up. There will be difficulties along the way to disrupting industries, but the payoff could be huge.

Learning about the traits of established industries can help you spot potential areas for change. Entrepreneurs can find uncharted areas for innovation by being aware of industry gaps, taking advantage of technological advances, and monitoring shifts in consumer behavior.

Thus, entrepreneurs hold the keys to changing the game and disrupting industries. The results of their ability to spot prospects, propel innovation, and overcome obstacles can be revolutionary. Entrepreneurs can pave the way for dynamic, sustainable, and impactful industry disruption in the future by embracing ethical considerations, understanding the impact on industries and society, and staying attuned to future trends.

THE END